The Landscape of Susse

The Landscape of Sussex

AMBASSADOR

SALMON

Published by J Salmon Limited
100 London Road, Sevenoaks, Kent TN13 1BB

First edition 2000

Designed by the Salmon Studio

Copyright © 2000 J Salmon Limited

ISBN 1 898435 60 X

Printed in England by
J Salmon Limited, Tubs Hill Works, Sevenoaks, Kent.

Front cover: Morning Light, Bosham
Back cover: Bodiam Castle
Half title page: Cottage at Selsey
Title page: Cottages in Old Town, Hastings

Church Square, Rye

Introduction

The beautiful county of Sussex is one of the most interesting and distinctive in England; it is also one of the largest, being seventy-eight miles from east to west.

The topography of Sussex is defined by several distinct areas of landscape. Much the largest of these, covering more than half the county, is the Weald, a picturesque belt of wooded hills crossing North Sussex with its highest point at 792 feet Crowborough Beacon. This was once the "Black Country" of England, where the iron industry was located, and up to the middle of the 18th century was bustling with activity. South of the Weald is a narrow, fertile strip of Greensand, on which many of the prettiest old villages lie. Then comes the magnificent line of the South Downs; hump-backed, bare and almost uninhabited. Below the Downs is the coastal plain where the resorts of West Sussex stand; several miles wide at Chichester this tapers to nothing where the Downs meet the sea around the magnificent chalk cliffs of Beachy Head.

Relics of primitive habitation are scarce in the county for the Downs are bleak and the tangled Weald was inhospitable. In Roman times Chichester and Pevensey were important and at Bignor, close to Stane Street, is the largest Roman villa in England; it had over seventy rooms and was richly decorated with mosaics. The Normans covered the seaward approaches with castles at Arundel, Lewes, Pevensey and Hastings. Monasteries were also numerous in medieval times; those at Boxgrove, Battle and Michelham are the best preserved. From this period date the noble castellated houses at Bodiam and Herstmonceux and countless other fine half-timbered and tile-hung domestic buildings.

From later centuries the Sussex landscape is also particularly well endowed with fine houses and more especially with a number of superb gardens. There are the beautiful mansions of Petworth, Goodwood, Parham and Uppark and gardens at Wakehurst, Nymans, Sheffield Park and Leonardslee, amongst others, all noted for their dazzling spring and autumn displays of colour.

It is, however, as much for its tranquil rural character as for its well-known sights that visitors are drawn to Sussex and there can be few other counties which can boast such a plethora of beautiful villages. Many attract tourists in their thousands - Alfriston, Bosham, Amberley, Eastdean - whilst others, equally delightful but tucked away, reward the more leisurely traveller.

The ancient market town of **East Grinstead** has a charter which dates back to 1221 and several half-timbered Tudor houses stand among the more recent buildings in the High Street. Sackville College is a magnificent almshouse with a picturesque courtyard. It was founded in 1609 as a home for the poor and disabled by Robert Sackville, Earl of Dorset and Treasurer to Queen Elizabeth I. In the time of William the Conqueror **Horsham** was a manor of some importance and it is still surrounded by the remnants of ancient forests containing the hammer ponds which date from the height of the Sussex iron industry. Impressive St. Mary's Church, with its 175 feet high shingled spire, is an indication of the town's importance in the Middle Ages. It stands at one end of The Causeway, so named because it was built on wooden piles to raise it above the surrounding river marshes. The lane is lined with beautiful old houses, one of which contains a museum of local crafts and domestic items.

Sackville College, ▷
East Grinstead
◁ The Causeway, Horsham

Between the elevated heathland of the Ashdown Forest and the fertile River Medway valley lies **Hartfield**. The village street is lined with old inns and delightful brick, timber and tile-hung cottages and the church has an unusual lychgate and shingled spire. Not far away and surrounded by quiet lanes, **West Hoathly** stands in well-wooded countryside just west of the Ashdown Forest in the High Weald. Once a centre of the iron industry, the village has a number of fine old buildings including a part-Norman church, a manor house dating from 1627 and some attractive tile-hung cottages around an old inn. Near the manor house stands the 15th century Priest House. This splendid timber-framed building, roofed with Horsham slate, is now owned by the Sussex Archaeological Trust and contains a small museum.

◁ The Lych Gate, Hartfield
The Priest House, West Hoathly ▷

Ashdown Forest extends for some 14,000 acres and is one of many areas of great natural beauty in Sussex. This tree-lined lane at Coldharbour near **Wych Cross** is typical of the undulating heathland which characterises the fringes of the forest, interspersed with streams and woodland. To the south-west of the forest is Chailey Common and some claim that the ancient village of **Chailey** on the western slopes of the River Ouse lies at the centre of the county. This fine smock mill is a well-known local landmark and its distinctive cap is of a design which was typical throughout Kent and Sussex. The windmill was once a familiar sight in the English landscape but it is now increasingly rare and the continued existence of mills such as Chailey owes much to the enthusiasm of local preservation societies.

◁ Coldharbour near Wych Cross
Chailey Mill ▷

The attractive Wealden village of **Mayfield**, which lies eight miles south of Tunbridge Wells, has a fine main street with some noteworthy old buildings of timber, brick and stone. Among them is an outstanding Wealden hall-house known as Yeomans and a 15th century gatehouse which leads to the remains of a palace founded by St. Dunstan, a Saxon Archbishop of Canterbury. Parts of St. Dunstan's Church date from the 13th century and it contains a fine 16th century screen. **Sheffield Park Gardens** near Uckfield are now owned by the National Trust. Covering an area of around one hundred acres and including no fewer than five lakes, the gardens were laid out in about 1775 by landscape gardener Capability Brown. In the early years of the 20th century the original design was extended and transformed by the then owner and the gardens now contain one of the finest collections of mature trees and rare shrubs in Britain.

◁ The Churchyard, Mayfield
Sheffield Park Gardens ▷

HOUSE
&
GARDEN
OPEN
11·00-5·00
EXCEPT Thurs.

ENTRANCE

Burwash is a village of exceptional beauty which is spread out along a ridge between the rivers Rother and Dudwell. It was an important centre of the Wealden iron industry in the 17th century which acounts for the number of outstanding old houses, many of them built by the ironmasters, which line the wide main street. The village is best known for nearby Bateman's, home of Rudyard Kipling from 1902 to 1936. It was built as a farm-house in 1634 and with its charming gardens it is now preserved as it was during the writer's lifetime by the National Trust. In the grounds there is a working watermill and a rare water-driven turbine, installed by Kipling himself. Standing nearly 650 feet above sea level, Brightling Down gives wonderful panoramas across the Rother Valley. **Brightling Church** is notable for its dwarf tower and contains some interesting brasses. John Fuller, the eccentric M.P. responsible for several local follies and known locally as Mad Jack, was buried in 1834 in the churchyard under a pyramid which he designed as his tomb.

◁ Bateman's, Burwash
Brightling Church ▷

The splendid walls of **Bodiam Castle** rise from an artificial lake beside the River Rother substantially unaltered since they were first built in 1386 as a stronghold against possible attack from the French. Although badly damaged during the 17th century, the castle is one of the best examples of its type in the country and its exterior walls, with towers over 60 feet high, is in a remarkably fine state of preservation. To the south is **Battle Abbey**, built by William the Conqueror on the exact site where the Battle of Hastings was fought. It was consecrated in 1094 but is now mainly in ruins. The impressive gateway, however, is well-preserved and provides a fine example of the Decorated period. The largest remaining fragment of this once great abbey is the monks' dormitory which was built in the 12th century.

◁ The Gatehouse,
Bodiam Castle

Battle Abbey ▷

The tranquil little town of **Winchelsea** was rebuilt on the hill-top by Edward I after severe storms in 1250 and 1287 battered and finally destroyed the original town below. The resulting "new" town is a fine example of early town planning with ancient inns, and red-roofed, tile-hung, houses beautifully preserved in wide avenues lined by trees. **Rye** was once an important port, one of the original Cinque Ports but the harbour gradually silted up and it is now situated some two miles from the sea, overlooking Romney Marsh. Popular with both visitors and artists, this fascinating medieval town was walled in the 14th century and one of its sturdy stone gateways still survives. Many of the ancient streets are cobbled and contain a wealth of lovely old inns and houses. One of many quaint corners in the town is picturesque Traders Passage, so called because the Ship Masters used to live here and in neighbouring Watchbell Street.

◁ The Landgate, Winchelsea
Traders Passage, Rye ▷

Today it is a popular modern resort but **Hastings** was one of the original Cinque Ports and the Old Town, with its picturesque old houses crowded into narrow twisting streets, retains many of the characteristics of an old fishing village. Hastings possesses the biggest beach-launched fleet of fishing boats in the country and when they are not in use, the boats can be seen drawn up on East Beach beneath East Hill. Hastings was the site of William the Conqueror's first castle; famous as the landing place of the Normans in 1066, Nearby **Pevensey** has a recorded history which dates back to Roman times when the stronghold of Anderida was an important south coast fort. A considerable part of the massive Roman wall still stands, up to 20 feet high in places. Pevensey Castle was built by the Normans and formed a vital part of their coastal defences.

◁ East Beach, Hastings
Pevensey Castle ▷

Michelham Priory near Upper Dicker, dates from 1229 when a Priory was erected by the Augustinians on an older, moated site. Later, parts of it were modified as a Tudor farmhouse and it now contains an interesting collection of fine furniture, Sussex ironwork and old wagons as well as a forge and wheelwright's shop. The gatehouse, which stands astride the moat, was built in 1395 to protect the monks who had been one of the targets of the peasants' uprising of 1381. Magnificent moated **Herstmonceux Castle** was built in the 15th century for Henry VI's Lord Treasurer but lay in ruins for many years until restored in 1933. Situated in one of the prettiest spots in Sussex, some ten miles north-east of Eastbourne, it is surrounded by attractively laid out and colourful gardens.

◁ The Gatehouse,
Michelham Priory

Herstmonceux Castle ▷

One of the finest resorts in the south of England, **Eastbourne** has been fashionable since the days of George III when four of his children visited the town. Beautifully laid out, it is renowned for its popular bathing beaches, lively pier and many attractive parks and gardens. The colourful Carpet Gardens make a rich splash of colour beside the Grand Parade on one of the most imposing stretches of the town's three-mile-long seafront. It is one of the few resorts which still possess a bandstand where military bands perform during the season. Reaching a height of 536 feet, the spectacular cliff formation of **Beachy Head**, to the west of Eastbourne, attracts many visitors. At the foot of the cliff stands the 142 feet high lighthouse which was built in 1902 to replace an earlier structure and which is visible at night for up to 25 nautical miles.

◁ Beachy Head
Eastbourne from
the Wish Tower ▷

Renowned for its lively entertainments, arcades and restaurants, **Eastbourne Pier** was voted "pier of the year" in 1997. Designed by Eugenius Birch, it was opened in 1870 although work was not finally completed for some years after that. Between Eastbourne and Seaford the chalk downs reach the sea forming the spectacular sweep of rounded cliffs known as the **Seven Sisters**. Protected within the Seven Sisters Country Park as part of the Sussex Heritage Coast, they are divided by deep clefts which are all that remain of ancient river valleys and the springy cliff-top turf is popular with walkers. The most westerly of the 'Sisters', Haven Brow, is the highest, rising to 253 feet.

◁ Eastbourne Pier
Seven Sisters ▷

Many old villages of flint-walled and russet-tiled cottages nestle between the rounded flanks of the South Downs and none is more attractive than **Eastdean** with its old cross on the green. The church, which contains a curious old font, exhibits work of the 12th to the 15th centuries although its tower dates from the 11th century. This is a popular area with walkers and the paths which lead over the Downs or towards Birling Gap, a mile away on the coast, are well-used. From Eastdean the road climbs steeply to the hamlet of **Friston** with its attractive pond. St. James' Church, with its tiny bell-cote, dates in part from pre-Norman times and contains some impressive monuments and brasses.

◁ Friston Pond
Eastdean ▷

The pretty little village of **Alfriston** lies beneath the Downs in the valley of the meandering River Cuckmere. The Old Clergy House, which dates from about 1350, is a superb example of a Wealden hall house and has the distinction of being the first building ever acquired by the National Trust. Amongst the many other attractions of the village are the splendid 14th century cruciform church known as the "Cathedral of the Downs" and an ancient Market Cross, the only one surviving in East Sussex. The **Long Man of Wilmington**, a 230 feet high figure of a man carved into the chalk of Windover Hill near Alfriston, is the largest hill figure in Europe. Its origins are uncertain but it is believed to be pre-Christian and has been attributed both to the Romans and the Saxons.

◁ Old Clergy House, Alfriston
Long Man, Wilmington ▷

An attractive old town of steep streets and narrow passageways, **Lewes** has always played an important role in the history of the county. The medieval castle was built on the site of an ancient Saxon fort to protect the cleft in the South Downs created by the River Ouse and the ruins, surrounded by a 12th century shell keep, still stand at the top of the High Street. The views from the top of the tower extend into Surrey and include the Reigate hills. Although it is less than four miles along the coast from Brighton, **Rottingdean** retains something of the atmosphere of a village. Old Rottingdean runs inland and its narrow street, lined with attractive flint-built houses, opens out on to a little green with a village pond. A well restored smock mill stands on Beacon Hill behind the village. It was built in 1802 and it was this mill which was used as a model for the emblem of the publishers William Heinemann.

◁ Lewes Castle
Rottingdean Mill ▷

The historic village of **Ditchling** nestles on the downs in the shelter of 813 feet high Ditchling Beacon. There are many outstanding old buildings in the village, among them the Early English style church which is full of interest and numerous fine houses, many of them Georgian, some dating from the 16th century. Anne of Cleves' House, so called because it was one of the estates given to her as part of her divorce settlement, is an impressive brick structure on a timber frame. It has the overhanging upper storey which is typical of Tudor architecture and ususual external steps. A fine pair of windmills known as **Jack and Jill Mills** stand above the downland village of Clayton. The black tower mill, Jack, dates from 1866 and has a traditional "beehive" cap whilst the white painted wooden post mill, Jill, was erected in 1821 in Brighton from where it was dragged some 30 years later by a team of oxen to its present downland site.

◁ Anne of Cleves House, Ditchling
Jack and Jill Mills, Clayton ▷

A number of pretty little downland villages nestle in the wooded folds of the South Downs providing an attractive landscape for walkers on the South Downs Way. Picturesque **Findon** lies on the east side of the narrow Findon Valley behind Worthing. Surrounded by farming country and rich pasture for the popular South Down breed of sheep, the village has long been famous for its traditional sheep fairs. Findon's Early English church stands a little to the west of the village, separated from it by the road. Another outstanding church is found in the nearby village of **Poynings**. The beautiful Church of the Holy Trinity was built in 1369, contemporary with many other Sussex churches such as Alfriston. The mining of flint was at one time a major industry in this part of the county and the exterior of this fine building makes use of local dressed flints.

◁ The South Downs, near Findon
Poynings Church ▷

One of Britain's most elegant seaside resorts, **Brighton** is a town of contrasts: handsome Georgian terraces stand alongside modern shopping precincts, and colourful parks provide a background for the marina. The varied attractions of the esplanade, the pebble beach and the Palace Pier are all popular with holiday-makers while the unique Royal Pavilion attracts visitors all year round. Originally built as a farmhouse, it was reconstructed in exotic fashion by John Nash between 1815 and 1822 as a seaside residence for the Prince Regent. Built in the style of an Indian Moghul's palace with a dome, pinnacles and minarets, the interior is also lavishly decorated. The broad avenues, lawns and squares of neighbouring **Hove** have a charm of their own and its superb Regency terraces rival any found elsewhere.

◁ The Royal Pavilion, Brighton
Regency Terraces, Hove ▷

The attractive village of **Steyning** lies beneath the north face of the South Downs and has a history which dates from the time of Alfred the Great. The long main street is lined with old inns and picturesque half-timbered houses as well as a Grammar School which dates from 1614. The church, founded in 1110, is an outstanding example of Norman architecture. Delightful Saxon Cottage is one of numerous attractive old houses and thatched cottages in the village which reveal several centuries of architectural styles and many different local building materials. It stands on the edge of a small green surrounded by 17th century cottages. **High Salvington Mill** can be seen for many miles around from its prominent position on high ground behind Worthing. This fine post mill is more than 200 years old and on one of its beams there is a seal dated 1774, evidence of early insurance against the risk of fire. The central post of the mill was cut from an oak tree growing on the site, the roots of which are still in the ground. The mill has not been in regular use since 1897 but it is carefully preserved with all its machinery intact.

◁ Saxon Cottage, Steyning
High Salvington Mill ▷

From its position 603 feet above sea level, the pre-historic hill-fort of **Cissbury Ring** dominates the surrounding landscape. It is the largest and most impressive of the earthworks on the South Downs – a series of oval embankments which are in an excellent state of preservation. Both Roman and Saxon remains have been found here and the mine shafts from which flint was quarried as long ago as 2000 B.C. are still visible. The little hamlet of **Sompting** is famous for its church, dedicated to St. Mary the Virgin, which dates from the 11th century. The remarkable Saxon tower has an unusual roof with a gabled pyramid cap which is unique in Britain. It is of a type which has come to be known as "a Rhenish helm roof" because it was once a common feature of churches in the Rhine Valley. St. Mary's was granted to the Knights Templar in the 12th century and the square chapel which they built on the south side was later incorporated into the south transept.

◁ Cissbury Ring, South Downs
Sompting Church, Worthing ▷

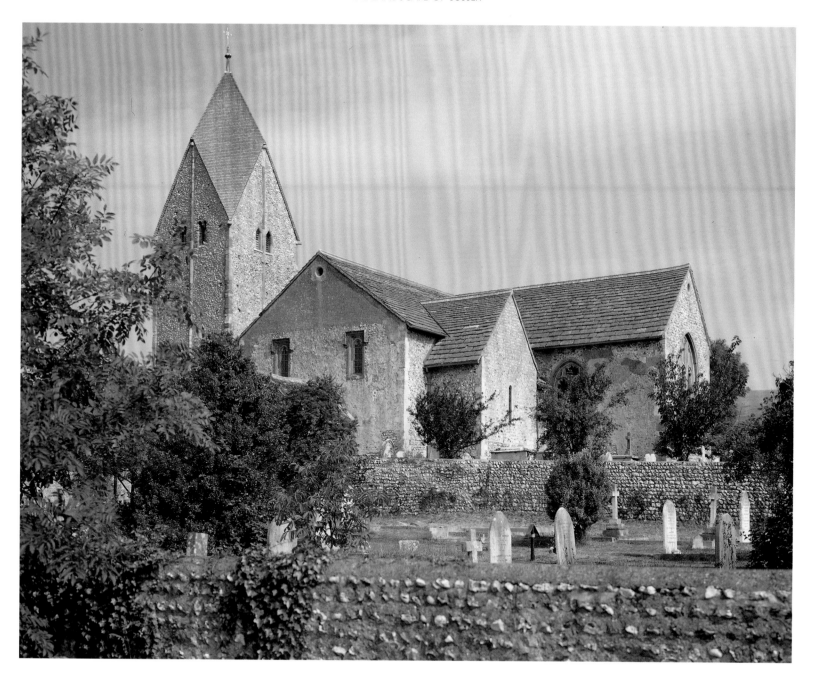

Situated to the south of Horsham, **Leonardslee Gardens** are among the most spectacular woodland gardens in England. The house, built in Georgian style in the mid-19th century, stands 300 feet above sea level overlooking a wooded valley. Against a background of traditional English trees such as oak, beech and birch, mixed with conifers, the gardens are particularly famous for their flowering shrubs which include camellias, magnolias and rhododendrons. Not far away stands **Shipley Mill**, a magnificent smock mill which dates from 1879. It is also known as King's Mill or Belloc's Mill having been owned by the writer Hilaire Belloc from 1906 until his death. The largest mill in the county, it has three pairs of stones and is noted for its double-shuttered sails. After Belloc's death the mill was allowed to fall into disrepair but in the 1950s it was restored as a memorial to the author.

◁ Leonardslee Gardens
Shipley Mill ▷

Built for the Duke of Somerset between 1688 and 1696, **Petworth House** is superbly situated looking across a lake and a great park which was landscaped in the 18th century. Past owners built up a splendid collection of paintings including works by Gainsborough and by Turner, who was a frequent visitor to Petworth, but it is for the Grinling Gibbons room that Petworth is especially known. Here there are some outstanding examples of the work of this famous wood-carver, including his unique fruit, flowers, birds and musical instruments. Five miles south of Petworth, near one of the largest Roman villas discovered in England, is the village of **Bignor**. It boats a number of attractive old buildings including the delightful 15th century Old Shop, once the village store, now a private house. This splendid timber-framed, thatched dwelling combines a stone foundation with criss-cross brickwork and solid oak doors reached by a flight of brick-lined steps.

◁ Petworth House
The Old Shop, Bignor ▷

Five miles north of Arundel in peaceful, rural surroundings on the eastern bank of the River Arun is **Amberley**, beloved by artists and frequented by fishermen. Here the stream flows quietly through green meadows past a Norman church and ancient thatched cottages and houses which exhibit a pleasing variety of styles and materials, reflecting the periods in which they were built. Amberley also boasts a ruined castle which was in fact a palace for the Bishops of Chichester. Some two miles away, but on the western side of the Arun, **West Burton** is one of a chain of attractive little villages which lie in the shelter of the hills, protected from the prevailing south-west winds.

◁ Cottage at West Burton
Cottage at Amberley ▷

Nestling in a gap in the Downs, the dignified town of **Arundel** is overlooked by the battlemented walls and towers of Arundel Castle. This magnificent fortress, set in a well-wooded park, dates from the 11th century and retains a Norman keep and gatehouse which give it an authentic medieval appearance. However, the castle owes much of its distinctive skyline to extensive rebuilding carried out in the 19th century. Arundel was an important settlement in pre-Norman times and comprises a fascinating mixture of old and new buildings, medieval streets and modern thoroughfares with many attractive corners and fine Georgian houses. **Bury** is one of a number of pretty little downland villages which lie in the fertile Arun Valley and Bury Hill is a notable viewpoint on the South Downs. It was in this charming village of stone-built houses beside the clear-running river that poet and novelist John Galsworthy chose to live and die.

◁ Arun Valley, Bury

Arundel Castle ▷

Founded in about 1117, **Boxgrove Priory** near Chichester is considered among the finest group of monastic buildings in England. It is commonly known as "the Cathedral of Sussex Parish Churches" and was used both by the Benedictines and by local parishioners. After the Dissolution of the Monasteries, half of the building fell into ruins but the superb Early English chancel remains. It was in the churchyard that one of the earliest recorded games of cricket took place. A mile to the north of Boxgrove **Halnaker Mill** commands a fine position high on the Downs near the village of the same name. With its distinctive "ogee" curved dome, the mill is the oldest of its type, built in about 1740 to grind corn for the poor of the parish and now restored to its original condition.

◁ Boxgrove Priory
Halnaker Mill ▷

A charming old market town surrounded by beautiful, unspoiled countryside, **Midhurst** is known for the famous polo ground at Cowdray Park and also for its connections with H. G. Wells who attended the grammar school here. South Pond provides a quiet corner in the town where there are a number of attractive 16th and 17th century houses as well as some fine old inns. The Church of Mary Magdalen and St. Denis still rings a curfew bell at 8 o'clock each evening as it has done for centuries since a lost traveller was guided to safety by the sound of the bell ringing. Set in the midst of beautiful Downland scenery the **Weald and Downland Museum** at Singleton is a fascinating collection of rescued historic buildings, workshops and exhibitions. Among the rural buildings reconstructed here are a medieval farmhouse, a toll cottage, a 16th century treadwheel, a forge, a village school and a working watermill.

◁ South Pond, Midhurst
Weald and Downland
Museum, Singleton ▷

One of Britain's oldest towns, the centre of **Chichester** still reflects the street plan of the Romans and retains many old buildings, notably from the Georgian period. The cathedral was begun in 1091 on the site of a Saxon church and is a pleasing combination of various architectural styles, centred upon its delicate, steepled spire. The original spire collapsed in 1861 and was rebuilt under the supervision of Sir Gilbert Scott. This is the only English cathedral to have a separate bell tower; it dates from the 15th century. The precincts are most attractive with flagged paths between ancient walls and many delightful secluded corners. The only Bishop of Chichester to be canonized, St. Richard de la Wych, has given his name to a walled passageway known as St. Richard's Walk which connects the cloisters to the cathedral close.

◁ Chichester Cathedral
Canon Gate, Chichester ▷

The delightful little village of **Selsey** lies to the south of Chichester on the peninsula which ends in Selsey Bill, most southerly point of the county. Now popular as a seaside resort, Selsey was originally a little fishing village and the area is of considerable historical interest since both Roman and Saxon remains have been found here. Crablands is one of the prettiest and best known of Selsey's many picturesque flint and thatch cottages, its name perhaps reflecting the fact that in the past Selsey was noted for its lobsters, prawns and crabs. At the head of one of the many creeks which together form Chichester harbour is **Bosham**, a picturesque old village and yachting centre which is reputed to be the scene of King Canute's encounter with the tide. Bosham's Saxon Church of the Holy Trinity is portrayed on the Bayeux Tapestry for it was here that Duke Harold attended mass in 1064 before setting out from Quay meadows on his ill-fated expedition to Normandy.

◁ Crablands, Selsey
   Bosham ▷

Index